A Grandmother's Heart

My Journey to Becoming a First-Time Grandmother

By

Debra Derenne

GRANDMA'S DREAM COMPANY
ARIZONA

Copyright © 2022 by Debra Derenne.

All rights reserved. No part of this book may be used or reproduced in any manner whatsoever without written permission from the publisher except in the case of brief quotations embodied in critical articles or reviews. For information, please contact *Grandma's Dream Company* at *deb19571@hotmail.com*.

Published by *Grandma's Dream Company* in the United States of America.

Derenne, Debra.

A Grandma's Heart: My Journey to Becoming
a First-Time Grandmother / Debra Derenne.

ISBN 9798833403341

First U.S. Edition 2022

Typeset and cover design by Fine Line Design.

Printed and bound in the U.S.A. by Amazon.com.

Dedicated to Miah, First Grandchild. Always remember that:
You are Smart
You are Strong
You have a Beautiful Heart

"I can do all things through Christ who strengthens me."
— Philippians 3:14

Dedicated to all the Mothers, Grandmothers, Fathers, Grandfathers and relatives of unborn children, that you may know that your unborn child is made in the image of God:

For You formed my inmost being;
You knit me together in my mother's womb.
[14] I praise You,
for I am fearfully and wonderfully made.
Marvelous are Your works,
and I know this very well.
[15] My frame was not hidden from You
when I was made in secret,
when I was woven together
in the depths of the earth.
[16] Your eyes saw my unformed body;
all my days were written in Your book
and ordained for me
before one of them came to be.
— Psalm 139: 13-16

CONTENTS

Acknowledgements vii

Introduction ix

2017 July 1

August 7

September 41

October 73

November 107

December 139

2018 January 173

ACKNOWLEDGEMENTS

A special thank you to a dear friend, Claire Hutchinson-Porter, of Ambassador Communications LLC, for her typing and editing skills, and her encouragement and wisdom in preparing this book for publication. You have made my dream come true.

I would like to thank a dear friend, Kenneth Johnson of Kenneth Johnson Photography of Arizona for the back cover headshot.

Thanks also to my loving, always supportive husband, Don Derenne, who walks with me on this journey.

Finally, thank You, my Lord Jesus Christ, for who You are, what You do, and what You give.

INTRODUCTION

I will never forget Mother's Day 2017, the day I was blessed to hear I was going to be a grandma for the first time. It gives me great joy for you to experience what I have experienced as a first-time grandma, the miracle God has given me to share this poetry with you. I wrote these poems starting from July 29th, 2017, up until the birthday of my first grandchild. God put on my heart to make memories of each day until her birth so that I can share this with my grandchild in the future. Becky, my sister at heart, once shared with me that having your first grandchild is a miracle, but being a first-time grandma is truly God's blessing.

My grandma's name was Eleanor. My mom's name is Ellen. My middle name is Ellen. Now I'm Grandma Elle. Grandma Eleanor was not only Grandma, but also my best special friend. Writing this poetry brings back great memories of my Grandma Eleanor.

Debra Derenne, June 2022

July ♥

2017

My Heart

Sweet Tiny Baby on your way,
May God keep you strong everyday.
I already love you from the start
Because you are taking a big spot
In my heart.

God's Plan

Sweet Tiny Baby
As you grow with God's Plan
You will have 10 fingers and 10 toes.
God will watch over you
That is for certain.
As you, Baby Person
Keep on birth-in.

Little Fart

Sweet Tiny Baby
In your Mommy's tummy
May you soon kick
And Mommy's tummy
Feel so funny.
Each little kick from the start
Will get even stronger as you fart.

August ♥

2017

Special

Sweet Tiny Baby
Good morning from God above.
Baby you are so special
And surrounded with His LOVE.

Chosen

Sweet Tiny Baby
Pink or blue, God is the one.
HE CHOSE YOU.
We are all waiting just to see,
Who you are and who you will be.

How Sweet

Sweet Tiny Baby
Pink and soft.
I can't wait to touch you
A whole lot.
Tiny little hands and tiny little feet.
MY OH MY!
Just how sweet.

Baby Bundle

Sweet Tiny Baby
Tucked in your Mommy's tummy
Tossing and turning
You must feel so funny.
As you grow bigger
Mommy's tummy will swell
And we will know all is well.

In Grandma's Arms

Sweet Tiny Baby
Sweet Tiny Angel Baby
Boy or girl, I can't wait to see you
Enter this world.
It's bright, it's dark, it's quiet, it's noisy
But Grandma's arms are warm and cozy.

Debra Derenne

A Miracle

Sweet Tiny Baby
In your Mommy's tummy
I got to touch you yesterday
Feeling so Grandma Elle.
Your Mommy says you feel
Like butterflies gentle and free
And you are a miracle
A BABY!

Baby, Your Ultrasound

Sweet Tiny Baby
Today Mommy and PaPa get to know more about you.
How you're growing and that you're safe and sound
In your little womb/room.
There are so many questions big and small.
Only God can answer them all.
These special pictures are your first ultrasound to see
How you're coming along.

Grandmas

Sweet Tiny Baby
Today both Grandmas met to talk
Grandma talk.
You are the first Grand Baby
For the both of us.
We are so…….! Excited.
I mean beyond WORDS.
Can't wait for you to be in both worlds.

Shining Star

Sweet Tiny Baby
Like a shining star
You are already brightening my life
Wherever you are.
May God point you into the arms
Of Mommy and PaPa, your FAMILY.
OH what a joyous day that will be.

Baby Seeds

To Sweet Tiny Baby
Size of a banana seed
Two weeks old
To chia seed three weeks,
Poppy seed four weeks,
Apple seed five weeks,
Sweet Pea six weeks,
Blueberry seven weeks,
Raspberry eight weeks,
Cherry nine weeks,
Strawberry ten weeks,
Lime eleven weeks,
Plum twelve weeks,
Lemon thirteen weeks,
Peach fourteen weeks,
Navel orange fifteen weeks,
Avocado sixteen weeks,
Pomegranate seventeen weeks,
Artichoke eighteen weeks,
Mango will come soon,
At nineteen weeks.
WOW...
How sweet you will be.
All from a baby seed.

Raindrop

Sweet Tiny Baby
Like tiny raindrops on your tiny head
Are kisses from heaven,
God Mommy and Dad (PaPa).
Each one is special as God has planned.
Just as He thoughtfully planned to have
Your Mommy and Dad (PaPa).

Rainbow

Sweet Tiny Baby
(God) morning Sweet Tiny Baby.
This morning as I was taking a walk
There was a beautiful rainbow
A gift from God
BLUE, PINK, and YELLOW.
You are such a blessing,
No matter who you will be
Baby Blue, Baby Pink, can't wait to see.

Sunshine

(Song)
Sweet Tiny Baby
Sunshine, Baby Sunshine,
You make me happy everyday.
You'll always know, dear
How much I love you
So keep growing
So I can see you play.
God will protect you
He really loves you.
He shows it to me EVERYDAY.

Baby Bump

Sweet Tiny Baby
As you grow
Muscles are forming
Head to toe.
Each little movement,
KICK, PUNCH, TWIST and ROLL
Will prepare you for
Your new world
When GOD SAYS GO!

Mommy, PaPa, and Me

Sweet Tiny Baby
Size of A (Artichoke at 18 weeks).
You have stolen my heart
Since you were a tiny bud.
You're still growing into someone
I already love.
Continue to blossom into
A person God made you to be.
With Mommy and PaPa you make three.

Baby is a Girl

Sweet Tiny Baby GIRL at 20 weeks birthing (Ultrasound Day).

Sweet Tiny Baby Girl
We found out today
Just what the pictures say.
Pictures are worth
A thousand words
And God planned you this way.
Mommy and Grandmas went shopping
Went shopping to plan your nursery.
Mommy and Grandmas see tiny pink dresses
Tiny pink shoes and tiny pink bows.
Pink tiny cheeks and pink tiny nose.

Tiny Senses

Sweet Tiny Baby Girl
Your five senses are developing:
Taste, hearing, sight, smell and touch.
Your PaPa has BIG MUSCLES
And yours are starting to grow.
So get the rest you need now
Because you will soon be on the go.

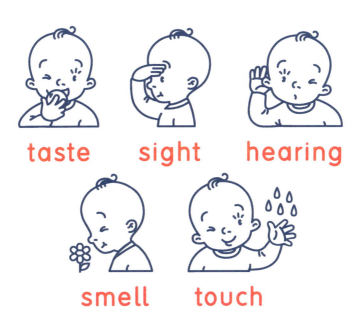

Joy

Sweet Tiny Baby Girl
As you yawn, hiccup, suck and swallow,
Can't wait until tomorrow.
As you grow, you bring us JOY
That only God can create.
We know JOY is from Jesus, Others, and you.
Thank you, Jesus, for all You do.
Amen.

Precious/Priceless

Sweet Tiny Baby Girl
Precious and priceless baby girl you are,
Our Princess
A heavenly angel coming from God.
Cherished you'll be with so much love.
No one can replace you at anytime,
Because God has made you one of a kind.

God's Creation

Sweet Tiny Baby Girl
10 tiny fingers, 10 tiny toes,
God even gave you
A pink tiny nose.
Tucked in your mommy's tummy
You tumble and roll.
Thank you, God, for blessing
Us with this beautiful BABY GIRL.

The Eclipse (2017)

Sweet Tiny Baby Girl
Today there was a solar eclipse.
The moon covered the sun for a few minutes.
The sky, sun, stars, the moon
Are gifts from heaven to you
That God will share with you
And as we look up to heaven
We thank God for you.

The Rocking Chair

Sweet Tiny Baby Girl
Rocka-Bye baby
In Grandma's arms
As I hold you tenderly
What a charm.
We will make memories
As we go
As we rock back and forth
Nice and slow.
So thank you, Jesus
For this precious baby girl
Through her tiny eyes
We will see the world.

Pink Balloon

Sweet Tiny Baby Girl
Pink is a color—delicate, sweet and cute.
Pink is also the color of a balloon
When we celebrate you!
The color of bubblegum is pink
Like cotton candy
And pink is the color of LOVE for many.
We celebrate you today
With this pink balloon
To show you just how much
We love you.

Birthday

Sweet Tiny Baby Girl
Today I went to Out of Africa Zoo with Sue.
I kissed a camel and giraffe too!
Just like a baby camel and giraffe
Are dated when born
You too are created and dated.
It's your BIRTHDAY
With many more to come
Starting with the first one.

Smile

Sweet Tiny Baby Girl
Today you are the size of a banana—20 weeks.
It's amazing to see you grow
From head to toe.
You bring a smile to me
Big and bright
Like a banana turned upside right.
So keep growing a whole bunch,
And giving Mommy's tummy a little punch.
As we wait
We will know that you
Still have time to grow and grow.

With Open Eyes

Sweet Tiny Baby Girl
With open eyes you will see
Many blessings there will be.
God has given you the sky, sun, stars and moon,
The rain, the thunder and even Boom.
Don't be afraid, because we are here
To love, protect you
And even cheer.
Love you to the moon and back, sweet tiny baby girl.

Family

To Sweet Tiny Baby Girl
Today, Mommy, PaPa, Great Grandma Ellen
Grandma Elle, Grand PaPa (Vic)
Auntie Brittany and Uncle Sam and I
Had Sunday lunch
Sat around the table and thanked God
A whole bunch.
We prayed for Mommy and Baby
Protection with blessings and God's direction.
When you join us, you will be
A true blessing to our FAMILY.

Precious Moments

Sweet Tiny Baby Girl
I'm thinking of you tonight
And what comes to me is an angel
So pure and white.
You spread your arms just like wings
And that allows you to do many things.
We will have precious moments
As you grow.
Hugs, smiles and laughter.
God told me so.

A GIFT

Sweet Tiny Baby Girl
You are such a GIFT
A blessing from God above.
You are a present
Not opened yet
Especially chosen
Such a gift.
God is getting ready
To give you to us.
Passing angels' arms
Through Him to us.

Grandma

Sweet Tiny Baby Girl
Call me Grandma Elle.
I hope you can hear me
From inside your Mommy's belly.
I can't wait to talk to you—rock you,
Read, play, and walk with you.
I'm so happy God is sharing
You with me.

Love Bug Hugs

Sweet Tiny Baby Girl
Hello Tiny Love Bug.
Big hugs, little hugs
Big hugs, little hugs
They all come from LOVE
One for each day from God above,
And many more are waiting for you
All from us. (TINY LOVE BUG).

September ♥
2017

F.R.O.G.

Sweet Tiny Baby Girl
<u>FROG</u> – <u>F</u>OR <u>E</u>VER <u>R</u>ELY <u>O</u>N <u>G</u>OD.
Is how I see it.
God is everywhere
Is how I say it.
God is with you as you grow.
God will always be with you
This I know.
Just like frogs jump and play
I too jump for joy today.

A Star

Sweet Tiny Baby Girl
Tiny miracle is what you are.
God gave you five points
Like a star.
You can
1. Taste
2. Smell
3. Touch
4. See
5. Hear
Close up.
Near and far.
Still waiting for you to come,
To see all the LOVE is yet to come,
And you are number 1. (Grand-baby)

A-B-C and 1-2-3

Sweet Tiny Baby Girl
Building blocks A-B-C
Building blocks 1-2-3
Tiny squares for tiny hands
Switching blocks from hand to hand.
Doesn't matter what you make
Because it's something you create.

PaPa's Pocket T-Shirt

Sweet Tiny Baby Girl
Your PaPa and GrandPa's Pocket T-Shirt
A small pouch sewn on a shirt
Like a small pouch you are in
Surrounded at birth.
It holds your heartbeats on PaPa's chest
While you're still at rest.

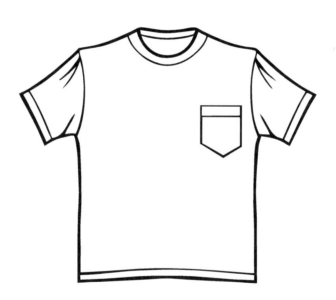

A Twinkle

Sweet Tiny Baby Girl
Twinkle, twinkle little star
Blessings, blessings, what you are.
From God's hands you have come
Down to earth to everyone.
Thank You, thank You for this babe—
From You, God
Specially made.

Baby's Growing

Sweet Tiny Baby Girl
Now size of a coconut (22 weeks)
Eyebrows still forming
Lips still blue
Ears hearing sounds from Mommy
And Mommy hearing from you.
Mommy's tummy is getting bigger
And so are her clothes.
When delivery time comes
God only knows.

A Morning Smile

Sweet Tiny Baby Girl
God morning to you, Sweet Tiny Baby.
The day is just starting
Bright and shiny.
The sun is rising
With a smile
From higher and higher
Many miles.
Your first smile will go straight to my heart
And there is no other way
To get a fresh start
In the morning.

A Blessing

Sweet Tiny Baby Girl
A blessing you are.
A gift from God.
Freely given for me
To LOVE.
He has chosen me
To be your Grandma E
And OH!
How proud of you
I'll be.

Baby Tear Drops

Sweet Tiny Baby Girl
Welcome to this world, Baby Girl.
As you enter
Tears will fall
Bringing happiness to us all.
This is a sign
We are waiting to hear—
Your first cry
And we will cheer.
This is a cheer
That will never stop.
All starting with
A tear drop.

Today

Sweet Tiny Baby Girl
Today is new, just like you.
New beginnings have just begun.
So much to see, so much to do.
So much fun for me and you.
Thank You, God
For laughter and play.
So many blessings
You give us today.

HAPPY

Sweet Tiny Baby Girl
You make me so happy.
Thinking of you brings
A smile to Grandma Elle.
Waiting to see
Your Angel face
So sweet and soft
Full of Grace.

Love

Sweet Tiny Baby Girl
Love you, Sweet Tiny Baby Girl.
Today, tomorrow, forever.
Love you, Sweet Tiny Baby Girl.
Born day or night
Only God knows what's right.
Love you, Sweet Tiny Baby Girl.
You make this a new world.

Tiny Tea Cup

Sweet Tiny Baby Girl
Tiny Tea Cup so pretty and fragile.
Tiny Tea Cup filled with love.
Tiny Tea Cup you are so special.
Baby girl you are so pretty (beautiful)
And fragile.
Baby girl you are loved.
Baby girl you are special
Created with God's hands from above.
Save a tiny tea cup
For you and me together
For our first tea
Filled with love.

Sounds

Sweet Tiny Baby Girl
So many things to hear
With your tiny soft ears.
Your Mommy and PaPa's voices come first
Since the beginning of your birth.
Voices, music, barking dogs
Car horns, raindrops, thunderous clouds.
Soft or loud
This noise will be
But always protected by your family.

A Baby's Breath

Sweet Tiny Baby Girl
Like a flower
You will blossom.
A baby's breath.
Like a flower
You bring beauty.
A baby's breath
Like a flower
You bring happiness.
Like a baby's breath
And happiness is
A baby's breath.

Butterflies

Sweet Tiny Baby Girl
Butterflies of many colors
Open wings that flutter and flutter.
Butterflies are beautiful
God's creation.
Butterflies change color with God's art
And God makes these changes
From inside His heart.

Fingerprints

Sweet Tiny Baby Girl
Fingerprints are special
One of a kind
That will last you
A very long time.
With each tiny finger
Five on each hand
You will touch
You will hold
You will play everyday
As you can.
And pray with Grandma Elle
Praying for Mommy and Dad (PaPa).

10 Tiny Toes

Sweet Tiny Baby Girl
10 Tiny toes (Piggies)
Cutest in the world
Just right for you
Sweet Tiny Baby Girl.
Your toes we will count
As they wiggle and tickle and play.
This little piggy is for Mommy.
This little piggy is for Daddy (PaPa).
This little piggy is for Grandma and GrandPa.
The tiniest toe is for Auntie and Uncle.
And all these piggies leave a footprint.

Size of a Grapefruit

Sweet Tiny Baby Girl
At 23 weeks
You are perfectly round
With tender pink cheeks.
These are cheeks
I'm waiting to touch
And even tenderly squeeze
Because I love you so much.
As I touch and tenderly squeeze
I want you to know
My love for you
Will grow and grow.

The Sky

Sweet Tiny Baby Girl
The sky is blue with white soft pillows.
The sky is white with a round dot of yellow.
The sky is dark with a white moon
And bright twinkling lights.
This Sweet Tiny Baby is when we say
Goodnight
As you fall asleep at night
Keep Grandma kisses all your life.

Heartbeat

Sweet Tiny Baby Girl
Heartbeat!
You have a piece of my heart.
Sweet tiny baby heartbeat
You bring me joy and happiness.
The beat of your heart
Puts a smile on my face
That nothing can erase.
Sweet tiny baby heartbeat
As you get stronger and stronger
Your heartbeat gets louder and louder.
HEARTBEAT.

Autumn/Fall

Sweet Tiny Baby Girl
This is a season with wondrous changes.
Leaves change colors
It's breezy and chilly.
You are the wondrous change in my life.
I became Grandma for the very first time.
Just like the changes still to come
God will be with you EVERYONE!

A Present

Sweet Tiny Baby Girl
A present is given
To show love.
You are a present
From God above.
You, Sweet Tiny Baby Girl, are a present
God gave
To share with loving care.
The day you are born
Is the present DAY
And then the future
Will be on its way.

A Cloud

Sweet Tiny Baby Girl
Way high up in the sky
Are white cotton balls
Floating by.
These are clouds
Floating freely.
All types, shapes and sizes.
Clouds bring rain, snow and ice.

Animal Crackers

Sweet Tiny Baby Girl
Animal crackers
In a box
Lions, tigers, bears and elephants
You'll love a lot.
Some from the circus
Some from the zoo
All will taste sweet as honey
Sweet like you.

PaPas

Sweet Tiny Baby Girl
You are so blessed.
You have a PaPa and GrandPa
And they're the best.
They are alike
In so many ways
And you will see it for yourself
Someday.
Most of all
They share their love for
You
Because that's what PaPa and GrandPa do.

Your Baby Shower

Sweet Tiny Baby Girl
Planning your shower
Harvest theme
With baby pumpkins
And everything.
Cut out cookies and pumpkin dip
Green punch and nacho chips.
Many more things
Your Mommy will eat
Especially the baby shower cake.
This baby shower
Is in honor of you
Beautiful Miah.

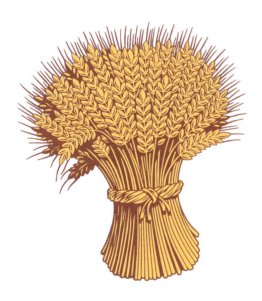

Cauliflower

To Sweet Tiny Baby Girl
Size of a cauliflower (25 weeks)
You know what's up
You know what's down
As your Mommy moves all around.
Your face is getting fatter
Your hair is growing
Longer and longer
And Mommy's growing
Bigger and bigger.

The Sound of Music

Sweet Tiny Baby Girl
Music is the sound
That fills the EARTH.
The sound of music
Is soft and loud
And heard at BIRTH.
Music is a melody
Music is a rhythm
Music is a collection.
Music is a beautiful sound.

First Friend

Sweet Tiny Baby Girl
Jesus is your first friend.
He loves you more than you know.
Jesus is a friend
Who will always be with you.
Jesus will always help you
Keep you safe and protected
In His own way.
So Grandma is praying for you
Until you learn how.
I bow my head
Join my hands
And pray to Him out loud.
Amen.

October ♥

2017

Anniversary

Sweet Tiny Baby Girl
Today is a special day
For Grandma and GrandPa.
It's our wedding anniversary.
We married 29 years ago
On a rainy day.
They say this brings you luck
On your wedding day.
Married at a park
White chapel
Horse and carriage.
I do's, a kiss—Then married.

Time

Sweet Tiny Baby Girl
It's not time
For you to arrive
Sweet Tiny Baby Girl
Still inside.
As you tumble
As you roll
Your Mommy's tummy
Still will grow.
January
Is your arrival date.
You may come early
You may come late.
Whatever time
You arrive
It will be
When God decides.

Reflections

Sweet Tiny Baby Girl
A reflection is when
You look in a mirror
And you see yourself.
You (are) a reflection of
Your Mommy and PaPa.
Your eyes, your ears, your nose,
And your face
Are all made
By God's loving grace.

Your Eyes

Sweet Tiny Baby Girl
At 26 weeks old
Your EYES are forming.
Soon they will open
Like a window
Sweet Tiny Baby Girl
And you will see the world
Sweet Tiny Baby Girl.
And with eyes blue, green or brown
You will look
All around
Especially when you hear
Mommy and PaPa sounds.

Shades

Sweet Tiny Baby Girl
Shades are coverings
That protect your eyes
From the sun and light.
Shades are of many colors
You might like.
Shades on windows
Go up and down
So you can see
What's all around.
You will learn
From what you see
With help and love
From your family.

Shapes

Sweet Tiny Baby Girl
Building blocks are square
Faces are circles.
Hearts are Valentines.
Valentines show LOVE.
Love comes in many shapes and sizes
Love comes from Heaven
Love's also on Earth
Love comes from all of us
Since your birth.

Feelings

Sweet Tiny Baby Girl
Feelings are happy
Feelings are sad
Feelings are normal
Even when you are mad.
Feelings of love
Are coming your way
Showering you
With hugs and kisses (soon to be your birthday).

Yellow Baby Blanket

Sweet Tiny Baby Girl
Your blanket is special.
Your PaPa came home
Wrapped in it
From the hospital.
It's as yellow as the sun.
It snuggles and warms you
And comforts you too.
That makes it even more
Special.
It's from Grandma Elle
With love to you.

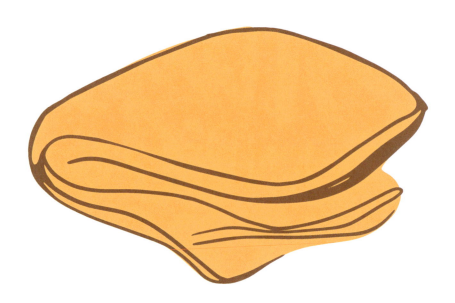

Music

Sweet Tiny Baby Girl
Music is a sound.
Music is a note.
Music is a lullaby.
A lullaby is a love letter
To listen and close your eyes to
And go to sleep
With a gentle touch
And a kiss on the cheek.

Lettuce ("Let Us")

Sweet Tiny Baby Girl
You are 27 weeks
And the size of a big lettuce.
Your lungs are developing
Your brain is active
You're getting smarter and smarter
And your hiccups louder and louder.
Soon you will be looking
Face to face
With your Mommy and PaPa.
So "let us" jump for joy
When you come
Because you will be
Baby number 1.
First-time Grandma.

Prayers

Sweet Tiny Baby Girl
Praying is talking to God.
He always shows His love.
God will listen to what you say
And answer you His way.
Never be afraid to ask
And receive
He will be so happy
Because you believe.
Amen.

Growing Up

Sweet Tiny Baby Girl
Puppies bark
Ponies neigh
Kitties meow
Cows moo
Birds sing.
These are a few
Of God's created things.
God made each one different
As He planned
As He did
Your Mommy and Dad.

Bubbles

Sweet Tiny Baby Girl
Tiny bubbles in your bottle
Tiny bubbles as you blow
Touch your lips, face and nose.
They will float in the air
Then POP! POP! POP!
Then they will stop.

Baby Rattle

Sweet Tiny Baby Girl
Baby rattle
In your hand
You'll shake, shake, shake
As fast as you can.
You will hear noises
Get louder and louder
As you shake it
Harder and harder.

First Road Trip

Sweet Tiny Baby Girl
On your first road trip
To Colorado.
Going to visit
Your Mommy's family.
Safe travel blessings
We gave to you
Mommy and PaPa too
Sending you off
On your way
Pray it's a clear
Sunshiny day.

Passing cars
On the highway
Leaves changing colors
And trees swaying
In the breeze.
You know what?
God created all of these.

Sunlight

Sweet Tiny Baby Girl
Today the sun is out.
The morning starts
With a bright light.
Children are playing
Dogs are barking
Birds are chirping
Car horns are honking
Then the day
Comes to an end.
The sun goes down
The light goes out
Tomorrow we start over again.

Leaves

Sweet Tiny Baby Girl
Leaves,
The season is Autumn.
Leaves fall
From the trees
Colors change
To gold, red, yellow
Orange and green.

Crunch is the sound you will hear
When stepped on.
Leaves make crunching sounds
Making it a lot of fun.

Debra Derenne

Baby Girl Hats

Sweet Tiny Baby Girl
Baby hats come in many
Sizes, colors, styles and fabrics.
Worn in different seasons
For different reasons.

Beanie hats, floppy hats,
Stocking hats, lacy hats
With pompoms and bows.
Many of them
Match your clothes.

Daytime

Sweet Tiny Baby Girl
Daytime is between
Sunrise and sunset
Light and dark
Day and night.

Daytime is sunshine
In the morning
Moon and stars at night.
So whenever you open or close
Your eyes,
Each day will hold
A surprise.

NIGHTTIME

Sweet Tiny Baby Girl
Nighttime is dark
Except for the shiny moon
And bright white stars.

Time to close your eyes
And have sweet dreams.
While you sleep
The angels from heaven
Will keep you safe
Until the next day
When you awake.

7 Days a Week

Sweet Tiny Baby Girl
Monday, Tuesday, Wednesday,
Thursday, Friday, Saturday, Sunday.
7 days a week to play
And have fun
With Mommy, PaPa
And everyone.

Special Days

Sweet Tiny Baby Girl
January is New Year's Day
February is Valentine's
March is St. Patrick's Day
And April is Easter
May is Mother's Day
June is Father's
July is Independence Day
When fireworks are flying.
August is Vacation and
National Friendship Day.
October is Halloween
November Thanksgiving
December Christmas Day
And January is extra special:
It's your birthday.

Angel

Sweet Tiny Baby Girl
How sweet you are.
You're adorable
You're precious
You are an angel
You are from God
From Heaven above
Sent with angel kisses
With much love.

Hands

Sweet Tiny Baby Girl
Hands are for touching
Holding and feeling.
Hands are soft and gentle.
Hands are for clapping
When you are happy
And when you celebrate
A special day
Such as your birthday.

Friend

Sweet Tiny Baby Girl
A friend is a special person
You will learn about.
A friend is someone special
As you grow.
A friend is someone
You have a relationship with.
A friend is someone
You really know.
A friend will tell you anything
And will trust you with everything.

Baby Sheep

Sweet Tiny Baby Girl
A baby sheep is a lamb
A ewe is her mother.
Your Mommy is your mother.

Everywhere your Mommy goes
(You) ewe are sure to follow.

Everywhere your PaPa goes
(You) ewe will follow too.

They will guard and keep (you) ewe safe
In every tomorrow
And whatever (you) ewe do.

The Moon

Sweet Tiny Baby Girl
Love you to the moon and back
Sweet Tiny Baby.

The moon comes out at night
And takes on its own life.
It's way, way up in the sky.

The distance to the moon
Is as endless as
My love for you.

Love you to the moon and back.

Rubber Ducky

Sweet Tiny Baby Girl
Yellow rubber ducky
Floating in the bath.
Over the water
Through the bubbles
POP! POP! POP!
SPLASH! SPLASH! SPLASH!
As your Mommy
Gives you a BABY BATH.

Baby Farm Animals

Sweet Tiny Baby Girl
Baby animals
In a red house.
This red house
Is a barn
On a farm.
A piglet, a lamb
A baby chick,
A pony and calf,
A puppy, a kitten
All grow up
As they're fed
In a house
That is red.

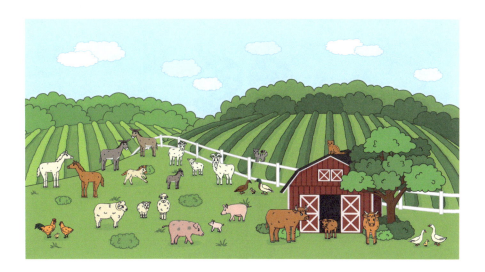

Baby's Movie

Sweet Tiny Baby Girl
Today you are 30 weeks strong
As you come along.
Numbers 30-40
Are what we see
As an ultrasound
Moves around
On Mommy's tummy.
We see your face
Your ears, eyes
And tiny nose.
We see your legs, feet
And 10 toes.
So until you're born
For us to see
We LOVED YOUR BABY MOVIE.

GrandPa Vic's Birthday

Sweet Tiny Baby Girl
It's Harvest Time
And GrandPa Vic's birthday.
It's all about pumpkins and candy corn
And honoring him.

We celebrate GrandPa Vic's birthday
Together.
Singing Happy Birthday for #60.

GrandPa Vic makes a wish
And here you are
Such a gift.
Thank you, God
For granting this wish!

November ♥
2017

Sweet Tiny Baby Girl

Sweet Tiny Baby Girl
Apple, Peaches, Clementine,
Mirabelle, OH! How fine.

All these fruits you see
Are fruits that are sweet
And from a seed.

Sweet Tiny Baby Girl
You are too
Sweet and so special.
This is you.

Funny Faces

Sweet Tiny Baby Girl
Funny faces you will make—
Sweet and sour with puff cheeks
Mommy and Daddy's (PaPa) faces too
Will be funny
When they PEEK-A-BOO!

Baby Bib

Sweet Tiny Baby Girl
A baby bib is a cloth
Worn over your clothes
To catch a drip and a burp.
They come in many
Sizes, patterns, colors, too,
Making it fun while you're eating.
So Mommy and PaPa have
Less cleaning.

Nursery Rhyme

Sweet Tiny Baby Girl
A nursery rhyme is a poem
A nursery rhyme is a song
A nursery rhyme is a short story
We can all be a part of.

A nursery rhyme is a lullaby
That will put you to sleep
And one of those lullabies
Will be counting sheep.

Lights

Sweet Tiny Baby Girl
When you open your eyes
For the very first time
You will see black and white
With blurry eyes.

As months go by
You will start to see
Colors of many kinds.

Shades of red,
Shades of blue,
Shades of green and purple:
These are some colors
Of Christmas lights
And they even sparkle.

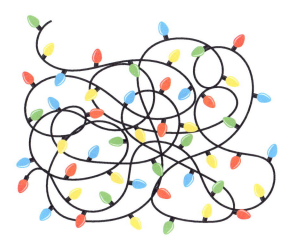

At the Park

Sweet Tiny Baby Girl
The park is a playground
Where children play.
As you grow you will
Go there someday.

Rocking horses, swings,
Teeter totters and monkey bars
You will see.
Making it a fun day
As you play with Grandma Elle.

Bumble Bee

Sweet Tiny Baby Girl
Bumble bees have stripes
Of black and yellow
And are our furry friends.
Bumble bees fly
From flower to flower
So baby bumble bees
Are born again.

Don't be afraid
If they get too close
And you hear a little BUZZ.

Just watch them fly by
In the sky
And send them off
With love.

Airplane

Sweet Tiny Baby Girl
Way up high
In the sky
Is an airplane
And like a bird
It has wings.

It flies fast
And makes loud noises
But don't be scared.

Look up!
Wave to the passengers
Blow a kiss and
Send them off
With love.

So they arrive
Safe and sound
Wherever they go
From the air above.

Baby Books

Sweet Tiny Baby Girl
Baby books tell
Your very first story
Of many different things.

Letters, numbers, colors,
Animals and cars,
Buses and people too.

Mommy, PaPa and Grandma
Will all read to you
Even when you go
To school.

Snow Man

Sweet Tiny Baby Girl
Snow falls from the sky.
On the ground it falls.
White, heavy for packing
Into two giant snowballs.
Another smaller for its head
The face it will show:
Two black coals for the eyes
Carrot for the nose
Sticks for two hands
Hat on the head
And buttons for its clothes.

A Christmas Stocking

Sweet Tiny Baby Girl
A Christmas stocking
Hung over the fireplace
Red and white
And even has your name:
Miah.

Filled with all kinds
Of surprises
That will bring you
Joy
With presents and toys.

Candy Cane

Sweet Tiny Baby Girl
A candy cane is shaped
Upside down
Like the letter J.

It has red and white stripes
And is sweet to taste
Even hangs on the Christmas tree
When you decorate.
The J is for Jesus
And Christmas is His birthday.

Balls

Sweet Tiny Baby Girl
Balls are
For you to have fun
Bouncing, rolling, catching, and throwing.

Many sizes, many colors
This you get to choose.

Using your eyes to see
Hands to catch and throw
Using your foot to kick
With so many places for it to go.

Hot Cocoa

Sweet Tiny Baby Girl
A chocolate
Mixed with water or milk
Tasting the best.

You drink it on a cold, rainy, or
Snowy day.
To warm your tummy up.
Marshmallows for snowballs
Floating on the top.

You will want to sip it
Very slowly
Because it's really hot.

A Thanksgiving Gift

Sweet Tiny Baby Girl
Everyday is a gift.
Thank You, Jesus, for Mommy and PaPa,
Grandmas and GrandPa Vic.
Thank You for my
Aunts, uncles, and friends.
Thank You for giving me
What I need and for even
Things I want.
But most of all, Jesus
Thank You for Your love.

Rocking Horse

Sweet Tiny Baby Girl
A rocking horse
Is what you sit on.
It goes forward and back.
It uses your tiny muscles
Your arms and legs.

You learn to balance
To be safe.
So hang on tight
So don't fall off.
Just giddy up and go!
And have some fun.

Mother Goose

Sweet Tiny Baby Girl
A book of fairy tales
And nursery rhymes.
A book to say or sing
Making many sounds and
Seeing many things.

With colorful pictures
And funny surprises
As you sit and read.
With quiet smiles and
Merry grins
To tickle your tummy.

Santa

Sweet Tiny Baby Girl
Santa is a jolly fellow
All dressed in red and white.
With a long white beard and
A wide black belt
That fits him very tight.

When he walks
He jiggles and wiggles
Every step he takes.

He wears a red hat
With white fur
With a furry ball on top.

With big black boots
On his feet
And a jelly belly
When he walks.

He gives a loud
"HO-HO and
Merry Christmas to all!"

Teachers

Sweet Tiny Baby Girl
Your Mommy and PaPa are first
All teachers help you learn and grow.
You learn letters, numbers, and colors
That you will see everyday.
SO
Don't be afraid
To ask any questions
Because that's how
You learn and grow.
Remember
Teachers always know.

This Little Light of Mine

Sweet Tiny Baby Girl
A candle on your birthday cake
Is to celebrate your life.
Year to year we celebrate.

Candles flicker while you
Wait to make a wish
Then blow it out.
We celebrate.

Keep this wish to yourself
So it will come true.
Let this little light shine
Just for you.

Babies

Sweet Tiny Baby Girl
Babies are miracles from heaven above.
Babies are a treasure
Priceless they are.

God planned for you
A long time ago.
Passed you down into
The arms of Mommy and PaPa to treasure.

Almost Thanksgiving

Sweet Tiny Baby Girl
Planning
Shopping
Cooking
For a special day.

Families together
Playing games.

We stuff our faces
Fill our tummies
Yummy
Yummy
Yummy.

We thank You, Jesus
For this food
And Your many blessings.

Thanksgiving Day

Sweet Tiny Baby Girl
Today is the day
For many thanks
We share around the table.

Today we create
Memories
And take a lot of pictures.

Thank You, Jesus
For the gift of
A baby to come.
And Miah is the one.

Magic

Sweet Tiny Baby Girl
33 weeks old this week
Your name is Miah.

It's a magical moment
When you are born.

It's a miracle
I'm waiting for
With all my
Heart
Mind
And soul.

Christmas Decorations

Sweet Tiny Baby Girl
Christmas bulbs
Christmas lights
Red, green, yellow, blue, and white
All put on the Christmas tree
To brighten up the night.
Santa's angels
Snowmen too
Guiding us through the night.

Candles

Sweet Tiny Baby Girl
Candles brighten the dark.
Candles are for celebrations.
Candles bring a glow
On all special occasions.

When you become
One year old
The first candle
You see
It's all yours
On your birthday.

American Flag

Sweet Tiny Baby Girl
A flag is a large piece
Of red, white and blue cloth
With 50 stars all about.
It's a symbol of our country
And our freedom.

Proudly we stand
Proudly it waves
Proudly to say
I was born in the USA.

Wheels

Sweet Tiny Baby Girl
Wheels are circles
In different and many sizes
That go round and round.

Wheels move on the ground
And in the air:
Airplanes, cars, trucks
Tricycles and bicycles.

All of these go and stop
And take you where you want.

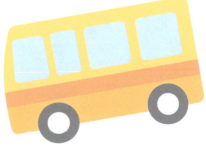

Toys

Sweet Tiny Baby Girl
Toys bring joy.
Toys bring fun.
As you grow
So does your imagination.

Some toys are quiet
Some toys are noisy
Some you pull
Some you push
And some you roll.

Use your imagination
As you go.

Christmas Colors

Sweet Tiny Baby Girl
Christmas colors
Bring a cheer
Telling you
Christmas time is here.

Many colors light and dark
Show their sparkles all about.

Colors you see
With your eyes
Are something special
A Christmas surprise.

December 2017

Miah

Sweet Tiny Baby Girl
Your name is Miah
Your Mommy and PaPa
Gave you that name.

It is special
Just for you
As are the stars in heaven
The sun and the moon.

To me you are
Radiant angelic
Exciting miracle
Indwelling Spirt of God
Adorable.

Christmas Songs

Sweet Tiny Baby Girl
Christmas songs
Are music to your ears.
Songs so jolly
Songs that give cheer.

All tell a Christmas story
Even one of Baby Jesus' birth.
Christmas is when Jesus
Was born in a manger.

(Jesus is the reason for
The season of Christmas.)

Jingle Bells

Sweet Tiny Baby Girl
Jingle, jingle
Is the sound
You hear
When moved or shaken.

Jingle, jingle
Is the sound
You hear
From Santa's suit
Santa's sleigh
And Santa's reindeer too.

Jingle, jingle
Will give you a smile
And a cheer when you think
Of Santa and his reindeer.

Christmas Tree

Sweet Tiny Baby Girl
Christmas tree
Tall and green
In a tree stand
Waiting to be decorated.

This is a special time of the year.
There is a spot
Waiting for you
Welcoming you
To our Christmas family too.

Baby Kick

Sweet Tiny Baby Girl
Today Grandma felt
Your Mommy's tummy
Waiting for you to kick.

What a miracle it is.

First time
Being a Grandma
And smile I did.

It makes you real
And that miracles
Come true
Only if you wish.

Christmas Candy Cane

Sweet Tiny Baby Girl
A candy cane
Red and white
A Christmas candy tradition.

It has a hook
Shaped like the letter J.
It hangs on the Christmas tree.

A special treat for you
And me.
It's a Christmas candy tradition.

Baby Pounds

Sweet Tiny Baby Girl
1 pound
2 pounds
2 pounds 3.
3 pounds 4 pounds
4 pounds 5.
5 pounds 6 pounds
7 pounds maybe 8
And even more if you're late.

Baby Book

Sweet Tiny Baby Girl
Take a look at this
Baby book and see
What Grandma Elle wrote.

A story before your birth
Waiting for you to come to earth.
You have been added to
Our family tree.

Welcome Miah
To this world
Where you will
Make Grandma so happy.

Cheeks

Sweet Tiny Baby Girl
God put cheeks
On your face
So we can gently touch
Gently squeeze and kiss.

Angel kisses
On your rosy cheeks
Are countless.

They come from Mommy
PaPa, Grandma, GrandPa Vic,
Aunt Brittany and Uncle Sam too.
This is a special way
To show you we love YOU.

HOME

Sweet Tiny Baby Girl
Home is where your heart is.
Home is where your family gathers.
Home is where LOVE
Continues to grow
Now and forever.

Changes

Sweet Tiny Baby Girl
Changes are coming soon.
You will leave Mommy's tummy
A warm and snuggly room.

Coming out into the world
We are waiting for you.

Don't be afraid.
God has you in His hands
And will hand you off
To Mommy and Dad (PaPa).

Baby Pumpkin

Sweet Tiny Baby Girl
You are the size of
A baby pumpkin.
Able to bend and stretch
Your arms and legs
At 39 weeks.

You are on your way
As you grow and grow.
Pumpkin is a cute name
Lovingly
We will call you.

Countdown to January 7th

Sweet Tiny Baby Girl
Your birthdate is around
January 7th.
You might come early
And you might come late.
God is the one who decides
Exactly your arrival date.
You are a
Growing miracle
Inside.

Christmas Table

Sweet Tiny Baby Girl
All around the Christmas table
We make memories.

Pretty tablecloth, dishes
And a candle red and green.

The candle in the center
Is lit for Jesus' birthday.

Ride Home

Sweet Tiny Baby Girl
Home sweet home
You will go
In the car
And on the road.

Buckled safely
In your car seat
With PaPa driving
And Mommy singing.

Light snowflakes
Falling like tiny stars
As we pass
Many cars.

Baby Alert

Sweet Tiny Baby Girl
BABY ALERT!

We are all waiting for that call.
Then we will know you're
On the way to the hospital.

There will be so much excitement
While we wait anxiously to celebrate you
BABY!

Christmas Cookies

Sweet Tiny Baby Girl
Christmas cookies
Fresh from the oven
Then on a plate.
With white frosting
Drizzled on each treat.

Santas, snowmen, snowflakes
And reindeer ready to eat.

Baby Bassinet

Sweet Tiny Baby Girl
This is for you.

When you close your eyes
And drift off to sleep
The angels fly over you
Cradled all in pink.

Baby

Sweet Tiny Baby Girl
Come when Jesus sends you.
Arms are open to receive you.
Mommy and PaPa are waiting
To hold you.
Come when Jesus sends you.

Baby Birds

Sweet Tiny Baby Girl
Baby birds in a nest.
Mommy bird
Watches and protects.

She loves them
Feeds them
Keeps them safe.

Teaches them
How to fly
North, south, east and west.

Little Red Wagon

Sweet Tiny Baby Girl
Little red wagon
With big black wheels
A long handle
To pull you up and down
Hills.

You will see many things
On your ride.
We say
Hello
Then good-bye.

A Guardian Angel

Sweet Tiny Baby Girl
A guardian angel
Is watching you.
A guardian angel
Will protect
And guide you
When Mommy and PaPa
Are out of sight.

Angel wings
So soft and white
When Mommy and PaPa return
Its wings will open and
Take flight.

A Picture of Nature

Sweet Tiny Baby Girl
Nature is the outside world
With plants, animals,
Land, water,
Moon, stars and sky.

Everywhere you look
You see
God's creations
With your eyes.

Christmas Eve Night

Sweet Tiny Baby Girl
We prepare for Jesus' birth
Gathering with family
And friends at church.
Candlelight services
Christmas song
Christmas trees
Christmas lights
Oh what a holy night.

Happy Birthday, Jesus

Sweet Tiny Baby Girl
It's Jesus' birthday
It's time to
Celebrate and live.

Love, peace and joy are what
Jesus wants
And what we can give.

Happy birthday, Jesus!

Birthday Cake

Sweet Tiny Baby Girl
A birthday cake is for a celebration
A birthday cake is a tradition.
A candle is added
For each year.

Make a wish.
Keep it a secret
Then blow the candles out.
Hush! Keep it to yourself
You're the one it's all about.

An Angel

Sweet Tiny Baby Girl
An angel is a spiritual messenger
Of God.
Known as a being of light.
Used by God to communicate
And watch over us.
A part of God's family with whom
You share your faith.

Mommy

Sweet Tiny Baby Girl
Mommy is another name
For Mother
A very special person.

She carries you from birth
Loves you unconditionally
No matter what you do.

A smile, hug, and kiss
Will always be there
For you.

Wake Up

Sweet Tiny Baby Girl
Wake up, wake up
Open your eyes
From a nap
You will arise.

Stretch out your arms
For a warm hug.
One is waiting for you.
You are loved.

The Old and the New

Sweet Tiny Baby Girl
This is year 2017 the Old,
2018 is the New.
2018 is the year
We are waiting for you.

New Year's Eve Night

Sweet Tiny Baby Girl
Once the clock strikes
Midnight
The New Year is here.
365 days make a year.
Only God knows how
This New Year will be
While we continue to count
Our many blessings.

January 2018

Happy New Year's Baby

Sweet Tiny Baby Girl
Happy New Year's baby.
It's 2018
You're still cozy and warm
In Mommy's tummy.
God will keep you
Safe and sound
Until she is ready.

Happy New Year, Baby Miah!

Picnic

Sweet Tiny Baby Girl
A picnic is
An outside meal
To share in the
Open air.
Sights to see
While you eat
And things you hear.

On rainy days
When PaPa and Aunt Brittany
Were little
We would throw
A blanket
On the floor
Eat and wait
To see a rainbow.

Move On

Sweet Tiny Baby Girl
Move on, move on
Soon you will be born
And headed in a
New direction.
Into waiting arms
Of Mommy and PaPa.
Face to face
You will see
What love means.

Baby Check Up

Sweet Tiny Baby Girl
Today we go see the doctor
For your check up.
To check your heart, nose, eyes and ears.
To check the heartbeat that she hears.

A thump thump
That is very loud
Tells her that your
Heartbeat is very strong.

Mommy and PaPa Are So Excited

Sweet Tiny Baby Girl
Mommy and PaPa are so excited
Waiting for you.
Waiting for that trip
To the hospital too.
You will be born
With the help of God's hands,
Doctors and nurses and
Many blessings.

Grandma Elle's Prayer to You

Sweet Tiny Baby Girl
Heavenly Father
Thank You for my grandbaby
I prayed before her birth
I prayed each day
That God would watch over her.

He will keep you close
And in His arms
And hold you tight each day.
As He does
I will continue to pray.

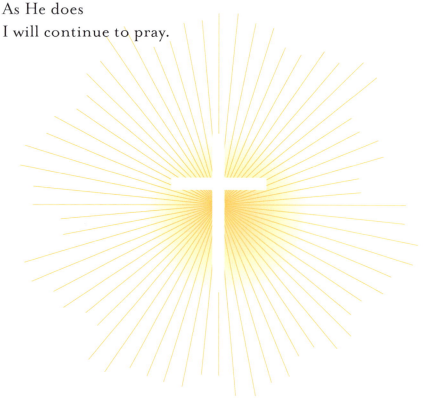

Happy Birthday, Baby
(Saturday, January 7)

Happy birthday
Sweet Tiny Baby Girl
Miah.

7 pounds
13 ounces
20 inches long

Blessed with 10 fingers
10 toes
A tiny button nose.
Chubby, rosy pink cheeks
And a face that glows.

Love Grandma Elle.

Manufactured by Amazon.ca
Bolton, ON